Ayurveda Health & Essential Oils

by Sandra Willis

1. How To Use This Book

This book will provide you with key information on Ayurveda Medicine and the role Essential Oils play within Ayurveda to deliver a wide range of health benefits. You will find this book is based on the following specific functions:

1. Provide you with valuable information explaining the history and purpose of Ayurveda medicine.

2. This book will detail the history and role of Essential Oils both in Ayurveda Medicine and throughout the world.

3. Provide you with information on how you can introduce Ayurveda medicine and Essential Oils to your life.

4. To explain the benefits, Ayurveda Medicine and Essential Oils can have on your life and health both on a short-term and long-term basis.

Ayurveda Medicine can be used to treat a wide variety of conditions and this book will deliver key information which will enable you to improve both your mind and body.

2. Introduction

Firstly I want to thank you and congratulate you for downloading Ayurveda Health & Essential Oils.

Nearly every culture in the world has incorporated essential oils in their history and traditions. Starting in ancient India and throughout Egypt, essential oils were used as medicines, cosmetic products, aromatherapy, and in many other ways. The medical discoveries made through essential oils have changed the medical world in many different ways; providing remedies of relief and cures to illnesses and conditions. Essential oils are one of the fundamental building blocks of holistic medicine even today, used by doctors and massage therapists around the world. The discoveries and advancements of plant oil usage are practically endless, as there are hundreds of different plants around the world, some still undiscovered. Learning about essential oils will not only teach you useful natural remedies but about cultures and religions from across the globe.

This book contains proven knowledge about the origin, history, and benefits of Ayurveda essential oils. As you journey through each chapter, you will acquire new information about the medical uses for Essential Oils and even how to make your own remedies to improve your everyday life. You will become knowledgeable on essential oils and how they have changed the world and deliver powerful benefits to your life.

Here's an inescapable fact: there are thousands of people diagnosed every year with a disease or condition, and then prescribed dangerous medicines with serious side-effects. But the fact of the matter is, before modern medicine, doctors used the earth's natural remedies to heal and treat patients with even the most severe medical issues. In today's world, holistic medicine is seen as some kind of joke or hippy-related nonsense.

For the thousands of years the benefits of Essential Oils have been utilized to treat a wide range of ailments, conditions and life imbalances. Essential oils were never meant to be left in the past; you can use them every day in your home and may even end up saving a life. However, you will need all of the information in this book to efficiently and effectively use essential oils. Without proper care and responsibility, a person can have critical reactions to their powerful mini-microbes.

If you do not develop your knowledge and skills of basic home remedies, then you are missing on the benefits of completely natural and powerful medicines and treatments. Treatments which can be used to treat everything from insect bites through to tackling Insomnia.

There may be critical times when a doctor cannot be reached or a friend is in pain, and understanding effective medical information to use natural substances can really help. Perhaps you are a mother with no medical background and your child is suffering from a bad burn? Or you have done everything you could to rid yourself from a bad chest cold and are in too much pain to sleep? But learning about essential oils is not just to become well-rounded with medical knowledge, it is to learn about an aspect of life that can benefit you in more than a dozen ways. And you will also learn their rich history as you begin your journey through these pages.

3. Ayurveda Medicine

"Ayurveda" is of Sanskrit origin, meaning "life knowledge" or "the science of life." Ayurveda medicine began in ancient India over four thousand years ago, with references to the medical usage of essential oils featured Vedic texts. Ayurveda medicine is based on a system of herbal essences that are similar to traditional medicine used in China which focuses on improving digestive regulation, meditation, yoga, removing toxins from the body, and psychological interventions. From the Ayurveda perspective, health is not just physical health or a lack of disease. Being healthy is radiating vigor and energy, which can be achieved through balanced food intake, stable sleep patterns, and other daily activities; all assisted by multiple treatments of various essential oil medicines.

Practitioners of Ayurvedic medicine believe that Ayurveda promotes disease prevention, individualization of medical care, and actively maintaining a balance between the spirit, mind, and body. In India, the Ayurveda approach to medicine and treatment is still considered incredibly important and is widely available throughout India and many developed countries. However, in Western society, including America and Europe, Ayurveda medicine is often shunned and instead paired with other treatments as secondary resources. However, Ayurveda medicine has been used to treat asthma, diabetes, heart disease, digestive dysfunctions, arthritis, and various chronic skin disorders.

Ayurveda treatments are delivered by doctors who are known as Vaidhyas. When a patient visits a Vaidhya, the doctor will spend most of the time evaluating the individual's overall health and resilience. They will even go through an assessment of the organ systems to make sure that they are functioning efficiently. As Ayurveda medicine is equally about the mind and spirit as it is the body, Vaidhya s will note deficiencies of both the physical and non-physical health of the person. The Vaidhya will make an assessment of the mental state and level of life-energy of the patients, and whether or not their environment is causing an imbalance. In India, there are over one hundred undergraduate colleges delivering courses in Ayurveda medicine, and thirty post-graduate universities. A degree in Ayurveda medicine can take several years to achieve. However, in the United States there are only a few colleges and universities that give students the opportunity to train in Ayurveda medicine. In fact, there is currently no certification process available or national standards in the field, which is why finding a well-trained and experienced practitioner is often is often difficult to achieve in comparison to India.

The first goal of determining treatments is understanding the patient's dosha. The dosha is a unique pattern of energy and living force that controls a range of activities within the body. Vaidhyas believe that health and illnesses are directly correlated with the balances of doshas in relation with one another. Identifying abnormal patterns of activity triggered by the bodies inability to adapt to a change in its environment and condition. Your body may suddenly experience an excess or deficiency, which can create illness and discomfort.

The initial treatment will primarily focus on balancing the dosha, which entails eliminating toxins from the body, improving digestive health, and changing lifestyle habits like diet, exercise, relationships, and stress levels. A Vaidhya will often prescribe herbal formulations with aromatherapy, aromatic massages, supervised fasting, meditation, yoga, and counseling.

There are certain branches of Ayurveda medicine that can be safely combined with common conventional medical treatments. There are even specific complementary and alternative therapies that are used in modern medical care. Many integrative experts in the United States incorporate Ayurveda healing treatments in their work.

In Western Society, essential oils are often treated a supporting resource for conventional medical treatment.

Women who are either pregnant or nursing should definitely speak with a health care professional before using any kind of essential oil, as well as before treating children with oil. The reasoning behind the concern is the contamination of toxins, like lead, arsenic, and mercury found in some Ayurveda remedies. Before applying Ayurveda remedies, you must make sure that the source of the essential oils is pure. When the herbal preparations are contaminated, there is potential for toxic substances to enter the body of the person using them. There are dozens of websites online which sell essential oils, without clarifying specific information about how they were prepared and if they are pure. First speak with an Ayurveda practitioner that you trust before purchasing or using any sort of essential oils for medical purposes. Alternatively only use Essential Oils which are clearly marked as "Pure" on the label. Some oils can be watered down or feature synthetic substances. However, Pure oils will consist of completely natural plant extracts.

4. The History of Essential Oils

Since the beginning of ancient times, the recorded history of plant life has given insight to rare and powerful essences and extracts that have been highly valued for their aromatic, therapeutic, medicinal, and even beauty enhancing properties. There are hundreds of plants that have been used as the foundation for many botanical and herbal remedies for thousands of years. These ancient medicines are the root of today's pharmaceutical drugs. The credit for creating ways to efficiently use aromatic extracts is commonly given to the Egyptians. However, the earliest recording of essential oil use dates back to the era of 3,000-25,000 B.C. It is believed that during the period that essential oils were first being used in Egypt, they were also being implemented in China and India as well.

Essential Oils in Egypt

It is believed that around 2,000 B.C., the Egyptians began using essential oils for spiritual enhancement, medicinal properties, and beauty regimens. The Egyptians became acclaimed for their wisdom of cosmetology and aromatic oils; incorporating essential oils into everyday life, especially those of higher status such as Kings and high rulers. The ruling families and priests of Egypt would wear the most expensive aromatic and perfumes. Pharaohs even had their own specialized mixtures for meditation, war, love, and other circumstances. The temple priests were doctors during that time, and would use an assortment of aromatic powders, balms, and oils in various methods for both medicinal and religious reasons. There are even illustrations on temple walls that show the royal families using essential oils.

One of the most well-known facts about ancient Egyptian essential oil preparations is that some were known as "Kyphi," with each blend consisting of sixteen different ingredients that were used for perfume and incense, and medicine. Some of the oils and resins from plants were converted into pills, suppositories, and medicinal cakes. Some of the most popular sources of oils were ashes and smoke from aniseed, onion, grapes, garlic, cedar, and watermelon. Specific scents were dedicated to each god and goddess; the statues of the deities were anointed with the oils by their devoted followers. Even in death the oils were highly valued, traces of cedar and myrrh have been found on discovered mummies with the oils used during the preserving process.

Essential Oils in Greece

Hippocrates, a Greek physician during the Age of Pericles, reportedly believed strongly in the medical uses of essential oils for aromatic purposes. Hippocrates is widely regarded as one of the most significant contributors to medical discovery. He believed that aromatic baths and scented massage delivered incredible medicinal benefits through fumigation. But above all other reasons for using aromatic oils, Hippocrates believed that oils and medicine can be used to provide to a natural healing energy to invigorate the bodies ability to treat and overcome a range of conditions and illnesses. The physician also recorded the effects of over three hundred plants, including saffron, cumin, thyme, and peppermint.   During 400-boo B.C., the Greeks recorded evidence of adopting essential oils from the Egyptians. Using aromatics and fumigation, the city of Athens was able to combat the plague.

One of the Hippocrates' peers, Theophrastus described the effects of aromatic perfumes, "It is to be expected the perfumes should have medicinal properties in the view of the virtues of their spices... they disperse tumors and abscesses and produce a distinct effect on the body and its interior parts." In Theophrastus' observations, he notes fundamental principles of aromatherapy, and how the external application of essential oils affect the internal organs and tissues.

Hippocrates' advanced wisdom of plants and their essences

originated in Ayurveda and was partly due to the Greek military's encounter with Ayurveda medicine while traveling with Alexander the Great throughout the Indian sub-continent. The soldiers would carry ointment myrrh into battle to protect themselves against infections. Another Greek who made vast advances in herbal medicine was Galen. Creating some of the first known records on how to classify plants and medicines, techniques which are still used today. Galen was also a surgeon for gladiators, and legend has it that no fighter died from wounds inflicted in the arena during Galen's time. Galen's grew to the point at he was made the doctor to one of the most popular Roman Emperors of all time, Marcus Aurelius.

Ayurveda Medicine in India

Although no one knows for sure exactly how old Ayurveda medicine is, it is widely considered that the practice has been around for at least four thousand years in India, and it is still practiced in India today. Records that date all the way back to 2,000 B.C. detail accounts of Indian doctors giving their patients oils of ginger, myrrh, cinnamon, sandalwood, coriander, and spikenard. When the Bubonic Plague started to enter India, Ayurveda was used to fight against it, replacing antibiotics that were ineffective.

India's most sacred book, the Vedas, mentions over seven hundred different aromatics and herbs that were used for perfumes, as well as for religious and therapeutic purposes. One of the widely used principle uses is an aromatic massage.

Basil, in particular, is one of the most sacred plants in India, and it is believed to have the ability to open one's mind and heart, insinuating energies of love and devotion. Similar to the Greeks, people of the Indian culture linked the use of their essential oils and plants to certain deities. Basil is a sacred in India and is considered to bestow healing, mental clarity, faith, and compassion.

Essential Oils in Ancient Rome

Many cultures used essential oils as medicine and to promote faith in their religions. However, the Romans used aromatic plants for decadence. People would bathe several times a day in essential oils, and frequently received massages to improve blood circulation and prepare for war. The Romans also used oils to scent the body, hair, bedding, and clothing. Throughout the Roman Empire there were incredibly skilled perfumers who would create new fragrances from newly discovered exotic oils harvested throughout the world and shipped back to Rome to be used by their leaders.

Although essential oils were mostly used for cosmetology purposes, the Roman army's doctor Pedacious Dioscorides used an impressive amount of herbal medicine in the first century A.D. Throughout the thousands of years since, his recorded remedies and methods have proven to be some of the most useful in the world. A few examples of his recorded prescriptions include: using myrrh to help fight gum infections, cypress to relieve diarrhea, and juniper berry as an effective diuretic.

Ayurveda Oils in China

The use of essential oils in China dates back to 2,6900-2,5900 B.C., to the reign of Huang Ti, regarded in Chinese culture as the Yellow Emperor. Huang Ti contributed to the medicinal use of essential oils in his book, "The Yellow Emperor's Book of Internal Medicine."

Another of the oldest surviving medical documents, Shennong's Herbal, dates all the way back to 2,700 B.C., and contains information on how the Chinese used more than three hundred plants. Shennong was a ruler of China and is considered to be a cultural hero of the country, who developed and taught the practices of agriculture. He himself ingested hundreds of plants and herbs to test their medicinal purposes. In fact, Shennong is said to have been the first person to discover tea and acupuncture and is considered to be the father of Traditional Chinese Medicine. Today, China is one of the world's biggest producer of essential oils.

Ayurveda and traditional Chinese medicines are some of the oldest forms of medicine around.   Both methods are instructional and focus on enhancing life, however, essential oils are more heavily used in Ayurveda whilst modern Chinese medicine focuses on the controversial use of animal tissue.

Essential Oils in Europe

Europe has one of the most extensive histories of Essential oils throughout the entire world. Starting in the Middle Ages, the Catholic Church claimed that using aromatics was purely for decadence. Although this idea set back the use of aromatics for therapeutic reasons, by the sixteen hundreds, texts about essential oils had become widespread across the continent. By the time the eighteen hundreds rolled around, most of the medical professionals in Germany, France, and England were prescribing and medicating patients with essential oils for a multitude of illnesses.

The south of France, home of many large flower growing districts, began supplying a variety of raw materials for French perfumers during the time when essential oils were being predominantly used for medical reasons. During the eighteen hundreds, tuberculosis was very common throughout Europe, yet the workers who processed flowers and herbs remained disease-free. The realization that essential oils within the plants being harvested were helping to protect the workers led to the first recorded laboratory tests of experimenting with anti-bacterial properties in essential oils in 1887.

In 1910, chemist Rene-Maurice Gattefosse made an incredible medical discovery while working in the lab. An accidental explosion in the lab caused his arms and hands to be covered in severe burns. To put out the flame, he submerged his arms in a large bucket of lavender oil. Gattefosse reported that simply rinsing his burns with the lavender essence completely stopped gasification of his body's tissue. The next day his burns had started to rapidly heal. This serendipitous moment let Gattefosse to further investigate the medical uses of essential oils by administering them to soldiers in military hospitals in World War I. He even went on to coin the phrase "aromatherapy."

Later during the 1980's, French doctor Daniel Pénoël and biochemist Pierre Fracnhomme analyzed and cataloged the medical properties of more than two hundred and seventy essential oils. Their findings were published in 1990, titled "L'aromatherapie Exactement," which became the preferred resource for other authors writing about the medical benefits of essential oils.

Essential oils have certainly withstood the test of time and proven their effectiveness on a variety of levels. Although holistic medicine is not regularly practiced, and even scoffed at by some in the United States, historical documentation provides verified insights and knowledge of how essential oils have been used in the past, and how we can use them to benefit our lives today.

5. Using Essential Oils

There are dozens upon dozens of uses for Essential Oils, all of which are widely used today throughout different cultures and for different reasons. In ancient Ayurveda medicine, the essential oil of a plant is called the "Agni," or fire of the plant. Researchers of Ayurveda pharmacology have found that the pure fire element extract of any plant is extremely potent and only a few drops can be used to treat specific ailments. The power of a plant's fire element extract is proven to be both dangerous and therapeutic. Using undiluted and raw essential oils as medicine can cause a range of hazards, including burning the skin or poisoning the bloodstream, leading to headaches, nausea, and vomiting. Overdosing on large quantities of undiluted essential oils can even cause kidney and liver failure. However, by mixing essential oils with carrier oils to dilute the potency of the essential oil they can be used completely safely to treat a range of ailments. With proper development and careful use, Ayurvedic substances can have amazing effects on the body, and even convert poisons to safe medicines.

Take a look through this chapter to explore the many uses for essential oils. From meditation to stress relief, to massages, essential oils can become a beneficial part of your everyday life.

Ambient Diffusion

Regardless of the state of your environment or home, essential oils can transform the entire character of a living or working space in just a matter of minutes. Many stores and online retailers sell aromatherapy diffusers or aroma lamps which disperse your favorite aromatherapy essential oil into the air, and in a variety of temperatures. Using essential oils to scent your home is ideal for purifying the air around you, along with creating a mood-enhancing atmosphere. Using essential oils to deliver aromatherapy can be used to treat pain, stress and anxiety along with enhancing energy levels, hair loss prevention and reduce symptoms of eczema. Essential oils deliver their properties through aromatherapy by delivering mini-microbes to the limbic system part of the brain which controls our most fundamental emotions ranging from stress through to pleasure. Accessing the brain via the olfactory system which is the sensory system used to provide our sense of smell. Ayurveda considers aromatherapy as an important method to prevent and heal a range of diseases and ailments. Traditional Ayurvedic treatments also use aromatherapy as a tool to support meditation and fumigation to purify the air. Essential oils can be used within Ayurvedic medicine individually to treat one specific condition such as insomnia or as a blend of a variety of different oils to treat both insomnia and stomach illness.

Massages

As you have previously read in this book, essential oils were commonly used for massages throughout ancient times, and still are applied today. It is said that a massage is the most favorable way to experience aromatherapy, because of the advantages of touch and relaxing aroma. As you may very well know, massages are given to relax muscles, as well as improve blood circulation, tone, and lymph flow. Combined with diluted essential oils, aromatherapy massages can help relax the person, create a relaxing mood, and make the individual smell great.

Ayurveda massage is used to treat the entire body, provide relief and support physically, mentally and emotionally. Traditional Ayurvedic text describe the use of a daily oil massage used to ward off old age, deliver improved vision, nourish the skin, support strong sleep and long life. An Ayurveda massage also targets the head, ears, palms and feet. Different to western massage styles which focus on the face and body. Ayurveda massage also incorporates a range of techniques including tapping, squeezing and kneading along with conventional strokes.

Ayurveda massage is designed to deliver a range of benefits:

- Detoxify and clean the body
- Boost the immune system
- Relieve stress and anxiety
- Improve blood circulation
- Increase mental and physical awareness
- Increase vitality and energy levels
- Support regular sleep patterns

Ayurveda "Abhyanga" Self-Massage

Ayurvedic medical treatments also include a form of self-massage referred to as "Abhyanga". Designed to provide personal stability and warmth the concept enables an individual to use an essential oil massage to saturate themselves with love.

To deliver an "Abhyanga" use the following steps:

1. Mix a single or blend of essential oils with a carrier oil and warm using a coffee-cup warmer. Test the temperature by adding a single drip to the wrist area of your inner arm. The temperature should be gently warm but not exceed this temperature.
2. Sit in a warm and comfortable room.
3. Rub a thin layer of oil to the palms of your hands and gently rub first the forehead with small circular strokes. Progress on to massaging your temple, face, and ears using upwards motions to build an emotional force to the brain.
4. With more oil applied to your palms use deep strokes on the arms and legs, continuing the circular motion in a relaxed and consistent pace.
5. Follow with a massage to the chest and abdomen. Around this area of the body push from center outwards to the kidneys and downwards towards the hips.
6. Finally, focus on the feet, using pressure on the soles of feet to deliver emotional feedback to release any remaining stress and tension.
7. Wash and rinse the oil in a warm shower or bath using

a thin of layer of soap to fully clean any remaining oils.

Repeating daily for approximately two weeks will deliver long-term emotional relief and personal warmth.

Skin Care

The key concept of Ayurveda skin care treatments is to cleanse, nourish, and moisturize the skin. When using essential oils always ensure that your skin is washed clean of dirt and dead skin cells. You can use a natural face scrub to exfoliate the skin, removing both dirt and dead skin cells. Adding essential oils on top of dirt will push toxins and germs deeper into the skin, embedding toxic elements into the skin and possibly the bloodstream. After cleansing your skin, you can add essential oils to your skin care routine by making facial oils. Simply mix two drops of your favorite oil with one large tablespoon of carrier oil, such as jojoba oil. Essential oils can also help open your skins pores through a facial steam; simply add one or two drops into a sink or bowl containing warm water, and hover your face over the water The steam from the warm water will rise the essential oils aromas and particles into the skin. You can also use your favorite oil mixed with a facial mask; simply mix facial clay, healing earth, or oatmeal with just enough water to form a smooth paste, then mix in two or three drops of the Essential Oil. Even a thin layer of the mixture will help to cleanse the skin and nourish the skin's cells.

Applying essential oils to the skin is referred to as 'topically'. The mini-microbes with essential oils enable the highly potent oil to penetrate the skin and enter the bloodstream. Therefore when applying essential oils topically it is important that the essential oil does not exceed any more than 5% of the total blended oil with the carrier oil. Similarly, you should have no less than 95% carrier oil blended with the essential oils. If you exceed more than a 5% dosage of Essential Oil then you pose the risk of poisoning the bloodstream or burning the skin. When using large quantities of oil such as an overall body massage then the dosage should be as low as 1%. It is important to remember that children's skin is less developed and much thinner than adult skin making it more absorbent to essential oils which can lead to poisoning the bloodstream. Therefore using essential oils on children should be avoided.

Bathing

Bathing in essential oils has restorative effects and has been considered a sacred activity since ancient Indian times. In ancient Greece, bathing was considered a gift from the gods to help cleanse the human body and restore strength. The Romans were first to build sunken baths not just in Italy but throughout Europe. However, it was the Indians and Ayurvedic medicine who first used essential oils as a cleansing agent. Ancient Ayurvedic texts provide insight into baths using honey, turmeric and milk followed by full-body oil massages and floral waters. The Ayurvedic bath was used to cleanse both the mind and spirit. Using essential oils in your bathing water can help relieve muscle strain, allay skin conditions, and improve emotional balance. Just add five to ten drops of essential oils mixed with a handful of bath salts in a full bath of water to allow the oils mini-microbes to safely enter the bloodstream and go to work.

Foot Baths

Foot baths are often used to pamper oneself, but they are also a perfect opportunity to use essential oils to relieve pain and reduce stress. Your feet have reflex points that influence each part of your body, passing messages to the brain which can treat a variety of conditions. The skin on your feet also absorbs essential oil quickly, helping to soothe aching joints or support blood circulation problems. Adding in three or four drops of oil into your foot bath with cool water can invigorate and energize your muscles while warmer water will sedate and relax them.

Chest Rub

Chest rubs provide a fast and effective way to deliver the benefits of essential oils when you are in a rush. Either at work or out and about a chest rub can be used to soothe respiratory infections such as colds and coughs or relax the mind thanks the rich aromas of your favorite oil. There are many products that use essential oils for their benefits for chest congestion. A wide range of oils are also recommended to help respiration and alleviate congestion. You can dilute around ten drops of rosemary, fir, or lavender in one ounce of carrier oil and simply rub the mixture on your chest, shoulders or upper back.

Insect Bites

Essential Oils feature a dual action for treating insect bites and scratches. Firstly essential oils can be used to repel a variety of insects and act as insecticides by overpowering the insects senses. Preventing them from biting you in the first place. Essential oils also feature anti-inflammatory properties which reduce redness, itching and swelling caused by insect bites. The analgesic properties can also relieve the burning and stinging pain triggered by an insect bite. Directly applying essential oils can alleviate itching, scratches, and insect bites. To help relieve skin irritation, you can dilute essential oil using a carrier oil such as aloe vera gel. All types of insect bites including horse fly, mosquito, and bee stings respond well to essential oils without the stinging pain may pharmaceutical products produce. Remember, when using essential oils topically they should always be used in a diluted form. Just a few drops of Oil can deliver powerful mini-microbes to the bloodstream.

Refreshing Mouthwash and Gargle

Essential oils feature a natural antiseptic and antibacterial properties which can provide a powerful and highly effective natural mouthwash. Essential oils will freshen your breath and help maintain gum health. Simply add two drops of the essential oil into a single cup of water, and swirl it around your mouth for a refreshed feeling. To make a mouth gargle from an essential oil, either to help heal your throat or a cough, simply mix the oil in one teaspoon of organic raw honey, then dilute the combination with enough lukewarm water to dissolve the honey. Your oil to water ratio should be one drop of water per one ounce of water. However, it is crucial not to swallow the mixture.

Misting

If you like your room or house to smell like your favorite plant or flower, just make your own mist. Misting is a very convenient way to add the captivating aroma of essential oils to your room and also to your skin. Misting also allows you to blend different oils in a single bottle. Misting bottles can be purchased from all good drugstores, health food stores, and some supermarkets. Simply add one drop of essential oil to every one ounce of water. In large bottles, you can add more oil to increase the aroma however the most effective method is to start small and to add more oil as you will be unable to remove the oil afterward if you have applied to much. Make sure to shake the bottle vigorously before each time you mist. You can also use misting on your pillow and bedspread to add a thin layer of relaxing and calming aroma before you go to sleep. The aroma will also continue to influence your olfactory system as you fall asleep. Providing a quick and simple method to relieving stress and helping to combat insomnia. A condition which is continuing to be proven to have a direct impact on peoples ability to control their weight.

Meditation and Yoga

Essential oils have been traditionally used in many cultures as a way to enhance spirituality, both religiously and non-religiously, for thousands of years. There are several oils that are well suited for meditation purposes, such as frankincense, sandalwood, myrrh, and patchouli. To apply them to your meditation ritual, simply burn the essential oil in a diffuser, or add a single of drop of oil in your hands and rub them together to inhale the sweet aroma.

One of the most powerful aspects of essentials oils is their flexibility, enabling oil to also be used as part of Ayurvedic yoga. The practice of Ayurvedic yoga utilizes the three doshic imbalances, Pitta, Kapha or Veta to relate specific Yoga sequences and postures to tackle different conditions and ailments.

A Pitta sequence will reduce the bodies heat using a range of respiratory postures.

A Kapha sequence will use to active and invigorating postures to increase the bodies temperature.

A Vata sequence will focus on relaxing postures to control excessive motion and stress on the mind and body.

Each dosha sequence is designed to resolve the most congested type of energy in your body, providing the most effective method of relaxing the body and treating an ailment or condition. Using an aromatherapy to add essential oil aromas to the air will strength the effectiveness of the Yoga whether it be to reduce stress or to tackle cold and flu symptoms.

6. Hydrolates

Hydrolates are a pure aromatherapy hydrosol, meaning it is the water that is gathered when the plant is steam-distilled for its essential oils, making Hydrolates much weaker than the highly concentrated essential oil liquid. Hydrolates are also known as flower waters and have a light aroma and soft nature. They are often used for people who require gentle care, such as children, the elderly, and sensitive skin types and skin conditions. One of the greatest properties about hydrolates is that they do not require dilution and can be directly administered to your skin.

Hydrolates are commonly used for:

- Soothing eye-pads and facial masks
- Sunburn relief
- Skin moisturizer
- Skin toners (for all skin types)
- To cool hot flashes
- To flavor natural yogurt
- Mist for home fragrances
- Compresses

Hydrolates originate from modern production techniques which are able to collect the condensation created when the plant material used to make essential oils are boiled and squeezed under huge amounts of pressure. It is unlikely that hydrosols were used during traditional Ayurvedic medical practices however they do provide a resource to use on sensitive skin.

7. DIY Homemade Recipes for Ayurveda Essential Oils

Ayurveda practices are specific methods in which aromatics, herbs, yoga, meditation, diet, and cosmetics are used to help keep balance in our lives. The ancient Indian science of Ayurveda is founded on the belief of an inherited genetic makeup and molecular biology; specifically treating different skin and body types based on the elements: fire, water, earth, air, and space. Now that you know more about essential oils, you can start applying them to your lifestyle on a daily basis. Improving your balance in life and your health. Massage therapy is the most effective way to experience the benefits of Ayurveda essential oils. Here are some useful homemade aromatherapy blends that use Ayurveda essential oils that are simple and take only minutes to make.

Ayurveda treatments featuring essential oils can be used to treat:

- Arthritis
- Stress
- Psoriasis
- Anxiety
- Muscular pain
- Circulation
- Back and joint pain
- Immunity
- Concentration
- Headaches
- Fatigue
- Dry skin
- Insomnia

Ayurveda massages can also balance your endocrine system, calm anxiety attacks, rejuvenate your skin, tone your muscles, detox impurities and toxins, lubricate your joints, increase alertness and focus, and stimulate your internal organs.

8. For Mental Clarity and Uplifting Spirituality

For this recipe, use either almond oil, coconut oil, or jojoba oil as the base carrier oil to dilute the essential fragrances.

Cinnamon Bark

Dosage: 5- 6 drops

Benefit: Cinnamon bark is a natural potent stimulant, with antimicrobial properties that promote digestive health.

Cardamom

Dosage: 3-4 drops

Benefit: Cardamom was traditionally used to invigorate the mind and body, as well as to ease nervous tension.

Coriander Seed

Dosage: 3- 4 drops

Benefit: the rejuvenating spice stimulates your senses, aids digestive health, and soothes inflammation.

Sweet Orange

Dosage: 14- 16 drops

Benefits: Sweet orange cleanses your mind, spirit, and body with an uplifting scent.

9. For Emotional Well-being and Increased Sensuality

For this recipe, use either grapeseed oil, olive oil, or jojoba oil as the base carrier oil to dilute the essential fragrances.

Clary Sage

Dosage: 2- 3 drops

Benefit: Clary sage will soothe muscle tension, relax your mind, and elevate your mood.

Bergamot

Dosage: 12- 14 drops

Benefit: Bergamot is fresh and spicy with a touch of citrus. It will help your muscles by relieving tension and elevating your mood.

Grapefruit

Dosage: 2-3 drops

Benefit: Grapefruit is fresh and tangy, and works by improving the health of your skin, promoting detoxification, and it contains antioxidants.

10. For a Relaxed Mind and Body and Help Sleeping

For this recipe, use grapeseed oil as the base carrier oil to dilute the essential fragrances.

These blends will help you fall asleep during a restless night. Simply massage several drops of the mixture over your temples, inside of your wrists, and your feet ten minutes before going to bed.

Sandalwood

> Dosage: 3- 4 drops
>
> Benefit: Sandalwood will soothe your mind and body, as well as work as an anti-inflammatory and decongestant.

Mandarin

> Dosage: 1- 2 drops
>
> Benefit: Mandarin is a light relaxing and cleansing oil that will also work as a digestive aid.

Valerian

> Dosage: 6- 7 drops
>
> Benefit: Valerian is a warm and powerful sleep aid that also reduces anxiety and lowers high blood pressure.

Lavender

> Dosage: 12 drops

Benefit: Lavender's sweet essence promotes relaxation while providing powerful anti-inflammatory benefits and detoxification.

Chinese Rose

Dosage: 3 drops

Benefit: Chinese rose is spicy, but relaxes your mind and body.

11. To Soothe Aching Joint and Muscles and Relax Your Body

For this recipe, use either grapeseed oil, coconut oil, or almond oil as the base carrier oil to dilute the essential fragrances.

The following blends will provide relief to sore limbs and joints. Enabling you to relax and recuperate after a heavy day at work or strong session at the gym.

Cajeput

Dosage: 13- 14 drops

Benefit: Cajeput is a fresh essence that warms your skin, alleviates muscle tension, and relieves pain.

Turmeric

Dosage: 13- 15 drops

Benefit: Turmeric is a woody essence that also has powerful pain relieving, anti-inflammatory, and antioxidant properties.

Clary Sage

Dosage: 3 drops

Benefit: Clary sage will naturally reduce inflammation and muscle tension while relaxing your eyes and mind.

12. Ayurveda and Aromatherapy

Around the world and over centuries of practice, the belief that essential oils have the properties to enhance self-awareness and spiritual ecstasy has led essential oils to become a staple in places of worship and meditation rooms. Essential oils like frankincense, lavender, sandalwood, rosemary, rose, angelica, and jasmine benefit the process of spiritual awareness and healing; balancing and strengthening your seven chakras.

Aromatherapy is the modern term for the ancient healing practice of burning strong smelling essential oils to enhance healing and meditation. The earliest recording of using aromatherapy dates back more than five thousand years to the ancient Vedic texts. When you breathe in essential oils, they flow to the part of your brain that influences your creativity, memories, desires, and emotions. Scents also help the production of certain hormones that control psychological and physical functions, so that your whole being is restored and rejuvenated. Applying diluted essential oils to your skin will allow the tiny molecules to enter through your pores and travel through your bloodstream, letting the vital mini-microbes within the oils positively affect your entire body, including your lymph.

Aromatherapy is a completely unique and personalized method of treatment; a scent that works for you may not necessarily work for someone else. Most often times identifying the essential oils that work for you can take a lot of trial and errors. Although the process may seem intimidating, Ayurveda has a variety of ways to help you identify the essential oils that will work best for you, taking into account specific factors like your mind-body type. The ancient Ayurveda health system in India explains that there are three forces in nature called Doshas. Doshas are continuously changing, which affects your inner balance. The purpose of aromatherapy is to naturally bring balance to your mind and spirit through the essence of plants. As we discussed earlier, the Ayurveda aromatherapy doshas that define aromatherapy practitioners are: Vata type, Pitta type, and Kapha type.

Vata Type

A Vata type individual is usually susceptible to dry skin, headaches, anxiety, stress, constipation, insomnia, and hypersensitivity. If you are a Vata type, you most likely avoid strong smells and perfumes. However, there are some essential oils that are warm and energizing to fit your needs: cinnamon, camphor, and cypress in particular. You can combine these essential oils with stabilizing and calming oils like jasmine, sandalwood, and rose. Simply mix two of your favorite essential oils with a carrier oil, like sesame, and use the combination for a relaxing massage or to breathe in when you are experiencing any of the common symptoms that are associated with Vata types.

The essential oils for Vata Dosha:

Amber, basil, angelica, bergamot, anise, camphor, eucalyptus, cardamom, frankincense, chamomile, coriander, cinnamon, ginger, geranium, lemongrass, jasmine, lavender, myrrh, patchouli, rosewood, rose, tangerine, sandalwood, thyme, vanilla

Carrier oils for Vata Dosha:

Sesame oil, avocado oil, and castor oil

Pitta Type

A Pitta type person usually suffers from anger, acidity, ulcers, fevers, inflammatory skin conditions, agitation, and ulcers. Therefore, a Pitta type may find peace through cooling and calming oil, like gardenia, mind, rose, jasmine, and sandalwood. Just mix one of your favorite flowery fragrances with a cooling carrier oil, like coconut oil, and rub on the undersides of your wrists, behind your ears, and behind your knees.

Essential Oils for Pitta Dosha:

Birch, chamomile, clary sage, brahmi, coriander, champa, fennel, jasmine, geranium, jatamansi, lemon grass, lemon balm, lime, lavender, neroli, mandarin, peppermint, myrtle, rose, spearmint, sandalwood, tea tree, tangerine, yarrow, wintergreen, ylang ylang, vanilla.

Carrier Oils for Pitta Dosha:

Coconut oil, olive oil, and sunflower oil

Kapha Type

A Kapha type individual typically experiences respiratory ailments. Therefore, they should use light and stimulating oils to find comfort; like basil, pine, cedar, and myrrh. Kapha types often benefit from strong, sharp fragrances. The slow nature of Kapha Dosha needs warming and cleansing essential oils.

Essential Oils for Kapha Dosha:

Angelica, basil, anise, birch, camphor, bay, cardamom, cinnamon, bergamot, cedar wood, clove, clary sage, eucalyptus, cypress, frankincense, ginger, fir, grapefruit, hyssop, geranium, juniper, lemon, jasmine, lime, neroli, myrtle, marjoram, peppermint, rosemary, petitgrain, sage, tea tree, yarrow, sweet orange.

Carrier Oils for Kapha Dosha:

Almond oil, grapeseed oil, and mustard oil

Ayurveda aromatic massages are used to deliver rejuvenation, health, and muscle therapy around the world, especially in India. In fact, a large tourism industry stabilizes the area around Kerala, where taxes and other incentives are geared towards entrepreneurs who want to build high-quality Ayurveda resorts that offer authentic Ayurveda treatment aromatherapy.

13. Ayurveda For Weight Loss

Ayurvedic treatments featuring essential oils can improve the bodies health and support weight loss without the side effects many modern drugs may deliver. Ayurvedic essential oils feature powerful properties which detoxify the body, support blood circulation, boost metabolism, control appetite and reduce cravings for fatty foods high in calories. The following oils, in particular, can be used via traditional Ayurvedic aromatherapy, meditation and massage to deliver weight loss:

Lemon Essential Oil: Lemon is an extremely refreshing oil which rejuvenates and revives the bodies senses using its detoxifying and energizing properties. Lemon also increases the metabolism function of the stomach, helping to break down fats and foods more effectively. Limonene, a colorless liquid found in lemon, supports the free movement of fatty acids throughout the bloodstream. Its aroma also uplifts the body and energy levels, promoting exercise and a healthy lifestyle.

Bergamot Essential Oil: Bergamot features calming properties which alleviate stress and anxiety. The calming effect delivers motivation and a sense of well-being, helping to reduce the cravings for excessive food.

Peppermint Essential Oil: Peppermint provides a powerful resource for treating digestive disorders in a fast and effective manner. Its powerful aroma can be used to control the appetite for food and directly impacts the senses which affect how full our stomach feels, preventing us from overeating and gorging on high calorific and sugary foods.

Grapefruit Essential Oil: This oil can be used to treat both cellulite and reduce the build up of fat cells from underneath the skin. It also acts as an appetite suppressant and supports the bodies ability burn excess fat.

Using aromatherapy along with Ayurvedic meditation provides a powerful method of relaxing the mind, reducing stress, providing a powerful healthy and natural alternative to consuming foods which are high in sugar as a method to relieving stress. To meditate simply fill the air with a warm and relaxing aromatherapy, sit in a comfortable seat or on the floor. Close your eyes and begin to take a number of slow, deep breaths. Breathing in through the mouth and out through the nose. Next free your mind of all stresses, as you do this you may think of solutions to your problems which enter your head. As you begin to meditate you may want to make a note of these using a handy notepad and then return to the meditation. However, your goal should be to clear the mind of all stresses and anxieties, leaving you in a refreshed and positive mood and without the need to gorge on food to improve your mood or to relieve boredom. Trying meditation for the first time can be a strange and bewildering experience but repeated use on a regular use can deliver powerful and life changing results to enable you to lose weight.

14. Quiz

1. In which country does Ayurveda originate?

2. In which country does aromatic aromatherapy originate?

3. True or False. Can a massage improve blood circulation?

4. What is Abhyanga? Self-massage, Aromatherapy or a form of Yoga?

5. Name the missing Dosha. Vata Type, Pitta Type and ...

6. Are Hydrolates less or more potent than Essential Oils?

7. When creating a massage blend what percentage of dosage should you not exceed when blending Essential Oils with a carrier oil?

8. Which country first began growing large volumes of Lavender to produce Lavender Essential Oil?

9. Do Essential Oils help to increase or decrease energy and vitality levels?

10. True or False. Essential Oils influence everyone in the same way?

15. Quiz Answers

1. India

2. Egypt

3. True

4. Abhyanga is a form of self-massage

5. Kapha Type

6. Hydrolates are less potent than Essential Oils

7. You should not exceed a dosage of more than 5% of Essential Oil when creating a massage oil

8. France

9. Essential Oils help to increase energy and vitality levels

10. False. Different Essential Oils can influence different people differently

16. Bonus Chapter: Panchakarma

Panchakarma is a program designed to cleanse and rejuvenate the body and consciousness. Improving the bodies overall health, the state of mind and self-healing capabilities. To reach the natural state defined by Ayurveda of well-being, happiness and health Panchakarma is used to detox the body, relax the mind, control the emotions and eliminate waste efficiently from the body.

In our modern world which delivers such high levels of stress and toxins to our body and mind, it puts immense pressure on our physical and mental systems. Wearing against our immune system and sleep patterns can lead to the accumulation of toxins and stress which can weaken our bodies systems to keep us in a healthy status. This weakening of our systems can eventually lead to the development of a range of chronic diseases ranging from depression through to cancer, obesity, and diabetes.

Panchakarma can help remove and reverse the negative elements in our lives which can damage our health and wellness. Cleansing the body of stress, anxiety and toxins. Helping to bring balance to our emotions and stability to our organs and bodily functions.

Panchakarma is delivered through a range of powerful and effective holistic treatments using completely natural therapeutic treatments. Each treatment is designed to cleanse the body and bring vitality and inner peace.

An effective Panchakarma treatment begins with an Ayurvedic consultation which identifies a patients existing health and pulse. The treatment process can be completed over a number of days and feature the following treatments:

Abhyanga which features a two-person oil massage

Swedana which is a personalized herbal sweat therapy

Shirodhara which is based upon warm oil being poured onto the forehead

Udhulana a herbal dusting which covers the body

One chromo therapy session

An effective Panchakarma treatment will also include Yoga classes designed to eliminate toxins, creating a therapeutic effect on the body. A Panchakarma Consultant will also monitor each individual stage, delivering an organic kitchari diet including herbal teas which support therapeutic treatments. The treatment will also deliver guidance for participants to continue their Post-Panchakarma experience in a healthy and relaxed state.

17. Conclusion

Thank you again for downloading this book!

I hope this book was able to help you to better understand Ayurveda Medicine and how essential oils can be used to deliver a range of health benefits.

The next step is to apply all of the information that you have learned in this book to your everyday life! Keep exploring your options for using essential oils and consider buying some to try out!

Finally, if you enjoyed this book, please take the time to share your thoughts and post a review on Amazon. It'd be greatly appreciated!

Thank you and good luck!

18. Disclaimer

Useful Websites

Along with www.esseentialoilsbookclub.com you can also use the following resources to learn more about essential oils:

http://www.beoa.co.uk – British Essential Oil Association

https://www.naha.org - National Association for Holistic Aromatherapy (USA)

http://airase.com - Association for the International Research of Aromatic Science and Education

http://www.a-t-c.org.uk – Aromatherapy Trade Council

http://efeo-org.org - European Federation of Essential Oils

http://www.ifaroma.org - International Federation of Aromatherapists

http://www.eoai.in - Essential oil association of India

http://www.thesma.org - The Association for Soft Tissue Therapists

http://www.iaim.org.uk - International Association of Infant Massage

http://www.alliance-aromatherapists.org - Alliance of International Aromatherapists